Cyber Security for Beginners

Everything you need to know about it (Cyber security, Cyberwar, Hacking)

Harry Colvin

Table of Contents

Disclaimer

While all attempts have been made to verify the information provided in this book, the author does assume any responsibility for errors, omissions, or contrary interpretations of the subject matter contained within. The information provided in this book is for educational and entertainment purposes only. The reader is responsible for his or her own actions and the author does not accept any responsibilities for any liabilities or damages, real or perceived, resulting from the use of this information.

The trademarks that are used are without any consent, and the publication of the trademark is without permission or backing by the trademark owner. All trademarks and brands within this book are for clarifying purposes only and are the owned by the owners themselves, not affiliated with this document.

Introduction

Organizations are finding it hard to achieve cyber security. Security in organizations is very important. It is through cyber security that customers will be able to trust the organizations they deal with. If sensitive information regarding customers is leaked to the public, the customers may lose their trust in the organization. The organization may lose customers, which might mark the beginning of its downfall. Governments should put all necessary measures in place in a bid to ensure that they achieve cyber security. For instance, they should stay protected against cyberwar, which can easily lead to physical war between countries. If a country perpetrates a cyber-attack against another country, the victim country may decide to seek revenge, which can lead to a physical war between the two countries. Some government documents, both soft and hard copies, carry sensitive information. If these documents are leaked, the global image of the country may change to negative. Only cyber security will help prevent this. This book is a guide on how cyber security can be achieved. Enjoy reading!

Chapter 1- What is Cyber security?

Cyber security refers to the process, technologies, and measures which are designed to protect networks, data, and systems from cybercrimes. With effective cyber security, the risk of cyber-attacks can be reduced and entities, individuals, and organizations can be protected from exploitation of technologies, systems, and networks.

The purpose of a cyber-attack is to expropriate information from an organization, individual, or public entity or to steal credit cards data, company secrets, customer details, or intellectual property. It also involves a compromise of official records, unauthorized access to networks, financial and reputational damage.

Recently, there has been an increase in cybercrimes. This is due to the following reasons:

1. Cyber criminals are indiscriminate- once they identify a weakness somewhere, they will try to exploit it. People are making multiple billions from cybercrimes, and that is why it has turned into a multibillion dollar industry.

2. Cybercrimes evolve constantly- the complexity of cyber-attacks is increasing every day, and organizations are struggling so as to keep up with this pace.

3. There are various forms of cyber-attacks- cyber-attacks are not designed to exploit weaknesses in technology only in outdated software but also to exploit people such as uninformed employees who usually click on malicious links. Some cyber-attacks are designed to

exploit organizations which lack processes and procedures.

Malware and Attack Vectors

There are various forms of malware and attack vectors used by cyber criminals to attack the targets. These include the following:

Malware is a software program which has been designed to enable criminals to achieve their goals. The following are the various types of malware used in cyber-attacks:

1. Ransomware- this is a malicious program which asks for payment once it has placed a cyber-attack on a particular computer system. It is a common type of attack for most criminals, and organizations are losing millions to it.

2. Viruses- this is a piece of code capable of replicating itself and migrating from one computer to another simply by attaching itself to other computer files.

3. Worms- these can also replicate themselves, but they don't need to attach themselves to a file so as to migrate from a computer to another. Their purpose is to look for vulnerabilities in the target system and report it back to their author after discovering any vulnerability.

4. Spyware/adware- this is usually installed on a particular computer after clicking on a link, opening an attachment, or after downloading an infected software program.

5. Trojan- this is a program which seems to be performing a particular function such as removal of malware, but it carries out an attack once installed.

The following are the attack vectors used by cyber criminals. They use them to attack computers with malware and then harvest stolen data:

1. Social engineering- this refers to the exploitation of the weakness of a particular individual by making them click on malicious links, or by gaining a physical access to their computer after deception. Examples of social engineering attacks include pharming and phishing.

2. Phishing- this is an attempt to acquire information from a user by masquerading to be a legitimate user.

3. Pharming- this refers to the process of redirecting traffic of a particular website to another different and fake website, where the information regarding an individual will be compromised.

4. Drive-by- these is opportunistic attacks against specific weaknesses in a system.

5. Man in the Middle attacks (MITM)- a type of attack involving a middleman between two communication endpoints. The middleman impersonates each endpoint and manipulates both victims.

Note that there are various ways that one can reduce the cyber risks, but it will be bad for you to think that you can achieve cyber security through technological implementations alone.

The three main approaches to cyber security include people, processes, and technology. For you to approach cyber security effectively, you should identify vulnerabilities, risks, and threats that your organization is facing, and then forecast the impact and likelihood of these to materialize.

After identifying the risks, the organization has to implement the necessary means so as to mitigate those risks, while ensuring a balance between the costs of the measures and the business objectives and the likelihood and impact of those risks occurring.

The good thing is that there are a number of risks which can help organizations to reduce the cyber risks they face. Organizations should take advantage of these frameworks and implement them as a way of preventing losses and inconveniences which result from cyber-attacks.

One of the problems facing cyber security is the quickly evolving nature of the security risks. Traditionally, the approach has been to harness most resources on the most sensitive system components and establish protective mechanisms against the big known threats. This way, the less important components of the systems were left unprotected and the less dangerous risks not prevented. If you consider this in the today's environment, this will be insufficient.

That is why advisory organizations are asking or promoting both adaptive and proactive approaches. Continuous monitoring as well as real-time assessments is recommended.

Cyber security requires a coordination of efforts throughout an information system.

The elements of cyber security include the following:

- Application security
- Information security
- Network security
- Business continuity planning/ Disaster recovery
- Operational security
- End-user education

Chapter 2- Application Security

Application security refers to the use of hardware, software, and procedural methods for the purpose of protecting applications from external threats. In software design, security has been an afterthought. However, security is becoming a very important aspect during the development of applications, as these applications are increasingly becoming accessible over networks, which makes them more vulnerable to different types of threats. The security measures built into applications and a good application security routine minimizes the possibility of an unauthorized code manipulating applications so as to steal, access, modify, or even delete sensitive data.

The actions which are taken in a bid to ensure there is application security are mostly known as countermeasures. The most basic approach to application security is by use of an application firewall which limits the handling of data or execution of files by some specific installed applications. In terms of hardware, a router can be used as a countermeasure, as it is capable of preventing the IP address of a particular computer from being directly visible when on the Internet.

Other measures which can be implemented for the purpose of ensuring application security include conventional firewalls, anti-virus programs, encryption/decryption programs, biometric authentication systems, and spyware detection/removal programs.

To enhance application security, one has to define enterprise assets, identify the purpose or work of each application in regards to the assets, create a security profile for every application, identify and prioritize the potential threats, and then document the adverse events and actions to be taken in every case. This process is referred to as *threat modeling*. A threat is any actual or potential adverse event capable of compromising an organization's assets, including malicious events such as denial of service attacks (DOS) as well as unplanned events such as a failure on the part of a storage device.

Choosing Application Security Tools

Delivering application security can be a challenge, especially when you are on a tight budget. This calls for you to be careful when considering your options. Priority should be given to the most critical assets.

Classify your applications and the data that they handle, and then classify them based on the order of their importance. Threat modeling can be used for identifying and evaluating the risks to applications, then taking the three top critical risks, and choosing the best way to remediate them. The kind of technology that you use will be determined by the requirements and objectives of your security policy, as well as the laws and regulations which are relevant to this.

Application white listing can be considered to be the best application security tool, since it provides the highest level of control over the user end-systems. Basically, white listing is just a default-deny model, and it works in the opposite way as the default-allow version of an antivirus model. The general concept in this case is simple, as only the approved applications will be allowed to run. However, this model has a problem, in that it may be difficult for you to have users accept that their tablets and PCs have been locked down.

Any product to be considered must be capable of automating the exception-management process and automate the list management process.

An application firewall is another way for you to implement application security. This tool can offer you protection against both emerging and current threats. Your existing firewall can even have all the capabilities which are needed. Some vendors for large firewalls usually provide web application layer protection in the form of an add-on module, and this helps in reducing the effort and cost required to have a second firewall. Installation of an application firewall is one thing, and managing it throughout is another thing. You must be sure that your administrators have both the time and the ability required to deal with log reviews and alerts. If your staff is capable of tuning and managing your application firewall, the additional costs can only be an incremental.

Application activity monitoring needs a log management product which will pull all the log information into a single place and then compares the entries from various places so as to come up with a holistic view of all the activity of the application. In some cases, the manual log analysis process is made impractical due to the volume of the log information. This calls for the need of automated log management to help in the process of correlating, aggregating, and reacting to the information captured in the logs across the organization. Due to the visibility provided, one can address the potential weaknesses proactively and be able to react more efficiently to security incidences.

A UTM (Unified Threat Management) device is an alternative to the patchwork of the individual single-function point devices, each one creating their own logs.

This normally gives a simpler network security model since its various services are designed to work in collaboration and at the same time be managed from a centralized console. This is good for saving money, time, and people, and this is why UTM is a very effective model in terms of day to day running costs. Due to a reduction in the number of hardware devices on the network, the number of vendors that you will have to deal with will also be reduced, and you will not have to have a very skilled IT department for day to day running of the security activities. Avoiding incomplete or conflicting rule sets as a result of misunderstanding about which products deal with which types of threats can consume a lot of time, even if the administrators are competent.

However, relying solely on a UTM has a disadvantage in that it will introduce a single point of failure, and when you consider the number of tasks that a UTM has to handle, scalability and network performance can be issues of concern, especially if the organization is large. Also, in case the UTM you are using does not have all the security features which are required to fulfill your security requirements, you will be forced to make an investment in some other types of devices. Also, you may have a good antimalware gateway, so you don't have to duplicate it with a UTM.

Whatever the application security device or software that you choose to use, it is advisable that you get evaluation copies of the potential products and then you deploy them in a test environment. Next, shortlist is the ones which exceed or meet your short as well as medium-term requirements. Also, you should ensure that these do not exceed or cost more than the value of your assets which need your protection and the expected cost in case a security breach occurs.

Chapter 3- Information Security

Information security refers to a set of processes which can be used for managing tools, processes, and policies which are necessary to detect, prevent, document, and even counter any threats to both digital and non-digital information. It is the responsibility of information security to come up with a set of business processes for protecting information assets regardless of how the information has been formatted, whether it is in transmission or not, whether it is being processed or it is being stored.

The information security programs are built for ensuring that the objectives of CIAD triangle are achieved, and these include integrity, confidentiality, and availability of business data and IT systems. Such objectives ensure that information is only accessed by authorized parties (confidentiality), the information is manipulated only by the authorized parties (integrity), and that the authorized parties can access the information at any time they need (availability).

In most organizations, a dedicated security group is created to create and maintain the information security requirements of the organization. The group in most cases is headed by a chief information security specialist. The security group is tasked with the responsibility of conducting a risk assessment, a process which involves assessing the threats and vulnerabilities to information assets. The appropriate protective controls have to be determined and then applied. Note that information is very essential when it comes to maintaining the value of an organization. If the organization stores its customer data safely, it will earn credibility and customer trust.

For attacks to be prevented and vulnerabilities to be mitigated at various points, a number of security controls have to be implemented and coordinated. This way, the impact of an attack is minimized. For the security to be ready for a security breach, they must have an incident response plan (IRP). With this, they can contain and limit any damage, remove any cause, and then apply the updated defense controls.

Information security policies and processes usually involve both digital and physical security measures so as to protect data from unauthorized use, access, destruction, or replication. Examples of such measures include encryption key management, mantraps, password policies, network intrusion detection systems, and regulatory compliance. A security audit may have to be done so as to evaluate the ability of the organization to maintain secure systems against a set of established criteria.

Chapter 4- Network Security

Nowadays, individuals and organizations are sharing very vital data across the networks. This is why network security is becoming part of every organization. It refers to any activity which has been designed to protect the integrity and usability of networks and data. Network security includes a combination of both software and hardware technologies. An effective network security plan is the one which manages how the network is accessed. It should target a wide variety of threats and prevent them from entering the network or spreading across the network.

There is no single mechanism which can be implemented in any organization and guarantee that the organization network will be secure. The techniques for network security keep on changing and improving with time as the attack and defense methods become more sophisticated.

Physical Network Security

This is an area of network security which is overlooked, and it involves protecting the hardware components from theft or intrusion. Organizations are spending huge sums of money so as to lock their network switches, network servers, and other networking equipment in facilities which are well guarded. Such measures may be impractically impossible in the case of homeowners, but it is highly recommended that households should keep broadband routers in private locations, away from house guests and nosey neighbors. If you are concerned about the theft of data via physical means such as stealing a router or a computer, you can solve this by avoiding storing your data locally.

Use online backup services so as to keep your sensitive files which are stored off-site in a secure backup location so that in case the local hardware is compromised or stolen, your files will remain secure in some other location.

The increase in the use of mobile devices has made physical security very important. Small devices can be easily forgotten in places such as hotels. They can also easily fall without being noticed by the owner. A small device such as a mobile phone can easily be stolen, even when you are using it. You must store your computer network equipment in safe places such as locked cabinets.

Password Protection

If passwords are used well and in the right way, they can help an organization to achieve network security. However, it is unfortunate that most individuals and organizations don't take password management with seriousness, so they end up using bad and weak passwords on their computer systems and networks.

The following are some of the password management practices that will help organizations enjoy cyber security:

1. Set strong pass codes or passwords on all devices which access or connect to the network.

2. Default administrator passwords for the administrator user should be changed.

3. Avoid sharing passwords with others. It will be good for you to set a guest network access for your friends and visitors if it is possible.

4. If your network passwords become widely known, change them.

In the case of strong passwords, it may be hard for you to remember them. If you avoid using them, keep them in a password manager.

Spyware

These are illicit programs capable of attacking both networks and computer systems without knowledge of passwords or without gaining a physical access. In most cases, this result after one has visited a malicious website.

There are several spyware programs in existence. Some of these programs will monitor web browsing and computer usage habits of an individual and then send this data back to corporations who will in turn use the data for the purpose of doing targeted advertising. Other spyware programs operate by stealing personal data.

A good example of a spyware program is the key logger, which normally captures and then sends all the keyboard keystrokes that a person makes. This is mostly used for capturing data about credit cards and passwords.

All the spyware running on a computer try to work without the people using it knowing, meaning that a substantial security risk is exposed. It is always hard for one to detect and remove spyware programs. This is why security experts recommend that we install and run anti-spyware programs on our computer networks.

Online Privacy

Identity thieves, personal stalkers, and even government agencies usually monitor our online habits beyond the spyware programs. When you use Wi-Fi hotspots from commuter trains and automobiles, your location can be revealed. Even in the case of the virtual world, the identity of a person can be tracked online via their social network activities and the IP addresses of their networks. Some of the techniques which can be employed so as to protect the identity of a person online include anonymous VPN services and web proxy servers. Although it is hard for us to achieve a complete privacy online, these methods provide us with some degree of privacy.

Wireless Security

Wireless networks have less security compared to wired networks. If you install a wireless LAN without the necessary security measures, you will have done the same as installing Ethernet ports everywhere including the parking lot. If you need to stay protected against exploitation by attackers, you must come up with devices which have been developed specifically to provide protection to a wireless network.

You must use the necessary security protocols when sending your data over a wireless network. Also, an organization must ensure that their data is encrypted before it can be sent over a wireless network. Organizations are also encouraged to filter the type of data that they transmit over their wireless networks. If the two parties are exchanging sensitive information such as passwords, they must first come up with necessary encryption and decryption mechanisms.

Chapter 5- Business Continuity Planning/ Disaster Recovery

A BCP (Business Continuity Plan) is a document with critical information which the organization needs to continue its operations in case an unplanned event occurs. This document states the basic functions of the business or organization, the processes and systems which must be sustained, and details regarding how to maintain them. The document should take into account any disruption which may occur to the business.

There are many risks which face institutions including human error, cyber-attacks, and natural disasters. These calls for businesses to have a business continuity plan which will help it preserve its reputation and health. If you come up with a good BCP, the chances of having a costly outage in your organization will be minimized.

The plan is normally created by IT administrators, but it is always good for the executive staff to participate so as to aid in the process, to provide knowledge and insights during its development, and to ensure that it is updated regularly.

Items of a Business Continuity Plan

The following are the items which should be contained in a business continuity plan:

1. Initial data, including the important contact information.

2. Revision management process which describes the change management procedures.

3. Purpose and scope.

4. Policy information.

5. How the plan can be used, as well as information regarding the time for initiation of the plan.

6. Emergency response and management.

7. Checklists and flow diagrams.

8. Step-by-step procedures.

9. Schedule for testing, reviewing, and updating the plan.

During the creation of a business continuity plan, you have to determine the best ways through which to deal with risks and threats so as to reduce the damage which may result from the occurrence of such events. A good business continuity plan is the one which outlines the step-by-step procedure for responding to events. It should also be kept current and updated through frequent testing and maintenance.

Disaster Recovery Plan (DRP)

This is simply a document written in a structured manner and defining the instructions to be followed when responding to unplanned incidents and events. It has the precautions to help in minimization of the effects of a disaster so that the organization can continue with its operations or quickly resume its mission-critical functions. This calls for the organization to determine the type of disaster recovery plan to follow in case of a failure.

Below are the various types of disaster recovery plans:

1. Virtual disaster recovery plan

This involves the use of virtualization technique so as to implement a disaster recovery plan in a simpler and efficient way. A virtualized environment is capable of coming up with new instances of virtual machines within minutes and then provide an application recovery via high availability.

2. Network disaster recovery plan

The plan for recovering from a network failure will become complex as the complexity of the network increases. It is good for you to come up with step-by-set recovery procedure, test it, and then keep it updated. Data in the plan should be specific to the network.

3. Cloud disaster recovery plan

This can be a file backup in a cloud or a complete replication. This type of recovery can be space, cost, and time-efficient but for you to maintain it, proper management will be required. The manager should be aware of where the virtual and physical servers are located. This plan should address the issue of security which is very rampant in the cloud.

4. Data center disaster recovery plan

This is a type of plan focusing mainly on infrastructure and a data center facility. One has to do an operational risk assessment when planning for this type of recovery, and you have to analyze the key components which include power systems, building location, protection, office space, and security.

Chapter 6- Operational Security (OPSEC)

This is an analytical process for classifying information assets and determining the controls which are required for protection of these assets. This is a process which involves five iterative steps discussed below:

1. Identify critical information

   In this step, you have to determine the data which will be extremely harmful once accessed by an unauthorized individual such as your adversary. This includes data and information about employees, financial statements, and intellectual property.

2. Determine threats

   In this step, you determine the persons who pose a threat to critical information about your organization. Your organization may have different adversaries who are targeting different information, so it is the work of the organization to determine the hackers or competitors who are targeting their data.

3. Analyze the vulnerabilities

   In this step, the organization has to determine the weaknesses in the safeguards it has put in place to protect the organization's critical information from adversaries. Any potential lapses in the physical and electronic systems of the organization have to be determined. Any area which leaves the organization's data and information exposed to attack is determined.

4. Assess risks

   After the vulnerabilities have been determined, you have to determine the level of threat which is associated with each of these. In most companies, the risks are ranked based on the likelihood of occurring and the extent of damage to be inflicted to the organization after the occurrence of the risk. In the case of highly pressing risks, the organization will be highly pressed to implement the risk management controls.

5. Apply necessary countermeasures

   In this step, you have to come up with measures to mitigate the risks, starting with those posing the biggest threat to the operations of your organization. Security improvements to be implemented should be determined in this step, and these include adding more hardware, more training, and even formulating new information governance policies.

In OPSEC, managers should view their projects and operations from outside-in, or from the position of their adversaries or competitors so as to identify their weaknesses. If the organization is able to extract their own information when acting as if they were an outsider, this is an indication that their adversaries can do the same.

Chapter 7- End-User Education

Users have a very critical role to play as far as organization security is concerned. This calls for the organization to deliver security awareness training and programs that will help deliver security expertise to the users and establish a culture which is security conscious within the organization.

Users have a very crucial role to play in order to ensure that the organization is secure, but they should be in a position to do their jobs effectively. If an organization fails to support its employees in providing the necessary security awareness and tools, it will be prone to the following security risks:

1. Removable media and personal devices
If there are no clearly defined policies regarding the use of removable storage media and personal devices, the staff may connect their devices to the organization infrastructure, which might bring malware or even compromise very sensitive organization data.

2. Legal and regulatory sanction
An organization may suffer from legal and regulatory sanctions if the users are not made aware and supported in the way they handle their sensitive information.

3. Incident reporting culture
If the organization does not come up with a proper reporting culture, then the users and the organization's security team will have a poor dialogue. A dialogue between the security team and users helps in uncovering the areas in the organization in which there is a need for an improvement in level of security.

4. Security Operating procedures

If the organization fails to balance the security operating procedures to support the way users perform their tasks, security may be seen to be a blocker and ignored completely. In case the users follow the steps carefully, it may damage the legitimate business activity.

5. External attack

Organization users have rights and accesses to the system of the organization, and they can be targeted for attacks. Attacks such as social engineering and phishing usually take advantage of legitimate user functions and capabilities.

6. Insider threat

The personal situation of employees usually changes with time, which may expose them to coercion. Such employees may release or give out organization's sensitive information to others. If an employee is not satisfied, he may abuse his system level privileges or even coerce other employees so as to access systems they are not authorized to access. Also, such employees may choose to physically deface or steal the computer resources of the organization.

Managing the Risks

There are a number of practices which you can put into place so as to counter the security threats targeting users. Let us discuss these:

1. User security policy

Organizations should come up with a user security policy to be part of the corporate security policy. All systems should have security procedures while considering the different business processes and roles. However, many organizations do not like to have a "one size fits all" strategy. Limited jargon should be used when describing the business roles and procedures.

2. Staff induction process

All new users, such as third party users and contractors, should be made aware of the rules they have to comply with to ensure that the organization is secure. The terms and conditions of their contract or employment should be well kept and maintained so that they can be used in case a disciplinary action is to be taken in the future.

3. Make users aware of the security risks facing the organization

All users should be trained regularly regarding the security risks that the organization is facing. You can create a platform where users will post questions regarding security risks and discuss the answers which are provided to them. Every user is in need of doing the right thing, so it will be good for you to provide them with the necessary advice.

4. Formal assessment of security risks

Staff members who work in the security department of your organization should be encouraged to enroll for courses about security of systems so as to validate and improve their skills. Some of the roles related to security such as system administrators, forensic investigators, and incident management team members may need some special training, so consider enrolling them for one for the benefit of your organization.

5. Develop an incidence reporting culture

The organization should attempt to develop a culture in which the staff is able to report any security incidences and malpractices to their seniors with no fear of being recriminated. The security team should also be able to take such concerns with a lot of seriousness and take the necessary actions so as to ensure that the organization is secure.

6. Monitor the security training process
The security training process should be monitored closely so as to ensure that it provides the necessary values to the trainees, who are your organization staff.

Chapter 8- Cyberwar

Cyberwar (cyberwarfare) refers to hacking which is politically motivated and it is carried out with a purpose of doing both sabotage and spying. Naturally, this attack is massive and is synchronized digitally so as to have a successful attack by a group or government against another.

Although cyberwar is an information war, its consequences can be similar to those of conventional warfare. Based on the effects of its use, it was found that there are no restrictions when using cyberwar. Examples of attacks categorized by security specialists as cyberwar include sabotage, information gathering, electrical power grid interference, and vandalism.

Cyberwar can be carried out by use of tools known as cyber weapons. The devices are simply basic programs created with the purpose of providing a strong defense or initiating an assault. Most of these cyber weapons can be found on the Internet. However, in the case of updated and complex weapons, they are kept privately by authorized individuals.

A cyberwar can become a real war quickly, with real weapons, and result into casualties. The cyber weapons cannot go far, but it is hard to control how they spread. Once cyber weapons carry out an attack, it becomes hard to trace the actions to the entity responsible for the act. This is because several proxies are used to infect the computers indirectly, which makes it hard for one to trace back the attack to any organization or malicious hacker. Even after you successfully trace the attack to a particular entity; it becomes hard to accuse a nation of deliberate act of war, especially due to the lack of legal frameworks.

The main problem is that we are living in a high-tech world where people are not well equipped and trained to handle such threats which can interfere with communications and network traffic moving to and from websites. Such attacks are capable of paralyzing Internet services providers (ISPs) at an international level and across national borders. This is why we should know how to handle cyberwar and cyber security issues as well as how to mitigate risks and minimize the damage.

Cyberwar Prevention

At a national level, it may be difficult for a country to protect its cyberspace. This is because of the number of connected computers, networks, and mobile devices. Most of the systems, including the ones protecting the critical infrastructures of the nation are interconnected, meaning that they are prone to both direct attacks and attacks resulting from transmissions. Additionally, the technology advancements are also a source of security risk because cyber terrorists always stay a step ahead in identifying security weaknesses in systems even before the security specialists can seal them. The difficulty in implementing boundaries and the lack of rules in cyberspace contribute to this.

Due to a lack of global response to cyberwar, most organizations and countries are creating task forces and structures for preparation against cyber threats. However, this alone may not be enough for us to stay secure from cyberwar attacks, so everyone should stay safe by securing their systems as much as possible. In the world fully connected through the Internet, every user faces either a direct or an indirect risk. The Internet provides many avenues for an attack, and this is why internet-connected systems should be secured globally.

Cyberspace is flexible, vast, and unregulated, and its users are prone to attacks from outsiders. The recent cyber-attacks have shown how information warfare techniques and tactics using computer connectivity pose a security threat in the exploitation of weaknesses caused by user inattentiveness or lack of good cyber security practices.

The most basic response to this is by use of firewalls, intrusion detection systems, and intrusion prevention systems. A real time network analysis should be done so as to detect such threats and contain them, and people will be able to detect simple hacking attacks at the user level.

In the case of large companies, they must know the vulnerabilities or threats to their network security and use Advanced Threat Protection Platforms so as to secure their properties for server security and endpoint protection.

In the case of cyber-attacks which are government-orchestrated, one of the mechanisms for staying protected is by creating a common front against the attackers. This is the time to start talks between various industries and the government so as to take the necessary action. Attacks carried out against large and interconnected systems may be easily disclosed by doing a data comparison and creating the common task forces. Using detection and prevention alone is not adequate for stopping attackers each time, but it may inhibit such similar threats in the future.

The increasing use of the Internet can be a weapon for terrorism, so for cyber vulnerabilities to be overcome, multiple different organizations should come forward to launch the cyber threats which can manipulate the physical world, as operations are done without international boundaries.

It is an unrealistic expectation that a single country will disarm its cyber arsenals on its own while the threats remain. This calls for countries to discuss and agree how to respond once one country is attacked by another via cyberspace. Without this, it will be easy for any country under a cyber-attack to begin bombing the suspect even before they can get the evidence to support this. If the countries of the world collaborate, they can come up with an enforceable cyberwar treaty. This way, the threat of cyberwar attacks will be minimized.

Chapter 9- Hacktivism

Hacktivism is a combination of two words, hacking and activism. It is usually done for a social or political cause. Local governments and states are finding themselves targets of hacktivism. Most cyber criminals usually hack into computers so as to steal data for cash, but hacktivists don't hack for cash. Hacktivists are just groups of individuals who come together to find injustice.

Hacktivists have gone after drug dealers, foreign governments, corporations, and pedophiles. Hospitals, police departments, small towns, states, and big cities have been attacked by hacktivists. The online activists have defaced websites, frozen government servers, and hacked into emails and data and this data has been released online.

Hacktivism has significant impacts on both local governments and states. It can deny the public access to government websites to conduct business or any other information.

Hacktivists are an unstructured group. They may be people who are not happy with a particular social injustice, and they are linked to social networks such as Anonymous, which is a very famous hacktivists group which attacks religious, government, and corporate websites.

There are various tools used by hacktivists. They sometimes hack into confidential records or private email and make them public. They sometimes compile individual information regarding targets such as police officers from government record breaches or the Internet, and this data is in turn posted online, a process known as *doxing*.

Such information can include the home address of an individual, their phone number, or the names of his children. The security experts will view it as harassment, while hacktivists will view it as transparency.

When the hacktivists need to launch a denial-of-service attack, they flood the website with traffic so as to knock it offline. To achieve this, they must gain control over a huge number of computers, by use of a malware program which is spread by sending an email with an attachment to the computer users. The malware is normally installed when a user clicks on a link leading to a website or when a user opens an attachment. The hacktivists then take control over the zombie computers. These computers are instructed to send traffic to a particular website so as flood it, and finally, it freezes.

If the number of visitors to the website exceed what it can handle, its server crashes. If a government computer system does not have any protections to block these types of attacks, the website will be knocked offline for some time.

The main goal of hacktivism is to create awareness about a particular issue, but most hacktivist campaigns usually go far to cause irritation or distraction, leading to loss of reputation, service disruption, and data compromises.

A good example of a hacktivist attack was the 2016 attack on the main website of the state of Michigan, where the aim was to create attention to the Flint water crisis. In May, North Carolina government websites were targeted so as to protest the controversial state law which required transgender people to make use of bathrooms which match the sex on one's birth certificate.

How to Prevent Hacktivist Attacks

The local governments and states should be prepared and ready to fight the online attacks including hacktivism. If the government computer systems do not have systems which can protect them against hacktivist attack, their officials should work together with Internet providers to install some programs which will help them block any illegitimate web traffic.

Such companies can also liaise with global cyber security companies which offer services to prevent massive assaults and do away with any bad traffic which is sent to the website and do away with any bad traffic.

States should come up with their systems which will help them thwart hacktivist attacks. Other mechanisms through which states, organizations, and local governments can stay protected against hacktivist attacks include the following:

1. Use of reputable virus detection and protection programs.

2. Monitoring accounts which face the public on Internet. Such accounts include social media, email, websites, file transfer sites, and others.

3. Any information identifying a person within the organization or the organization itself should not be made available online.

4. Update your defense programs and systems on a frequent basis so as to stay protected against potential attacks.

There is no single way for any organization or individual to stay protected against hacktivist attacks, but it is recommended that they should stay prepared to thwart such attacks as much as possible. It is worried that hacktivist attacks are becoming more complex, and the consequences of such attacks will become serious. Currently, citizens are sometimes barred from renewing their driving licenses and or there is a lack of revenue collection services. However, with time, hacktivist attacks could knock out water systems, the electric grid, and other utilities.

Chapter 10- Cyber-terrorism

Terrorism is any unlawful use of violence or force against property or persons so as to intimidate a government or the civilian population for social or political objectives. Cyber-terrorism is the use of computing resources to coerce or intimidate others. An example of a cyber-terrorism attack is hacking into a hospital system and changing the medical prescription of an individual so as to obtain revenge.

Anyone can get instructions on how to exploit a computer from the Internet. The process of identifying the initiators of the cyber-attacks is very hard. This is brought about by the fact that commercial enterprises are not willing to report the attacks due to concerns to do with liability.

With the increase in the number of cyber-attacks carried out worldwide, the data obtained from such attacks can accurately be used to show the individuals are who initiated the attack, whether a terrorism-sponsoring state or a terrorist group.

Research has shown that most cyber-attacks are mostly directed towards critical infrastructure industry companies. Research has also shown that there is an increase in the number of successful cyber-attacks on Data Acquisition and infrastructure Supervisory Control systems. The number of attacks attempting to intrude into the military networks has also increased. However, there are no clear explanations on the effects of these attacks on the military operations.

Cyber-terrorism attacks can result into a severe damage to the economy. However, in the United States, the recovery can be easily done.

A cyber-terrorism attack can also destroy a state's financial market. Other states which rely on the economy can also be affected.

There is no secure way through which you can stay protected against cyber-terrorism. In the military, sensitive information is stored in computers which are not connected to the world through the Internet. This is a good way to stay protected against cyber-terrorism. Encryption is also another way for an organization to protect them against cyber terrorism. However, the problem with encryption is that it does not protect the whole system. If any attack is geared towards crippling the whole system, for example, a virus, then encryption will not protect one against such an attack.

Firewalls can also be used to check and screen all the communications which get to a system including the e-mail messages. A firewall is simply a method of filtering any access to a network. These methods can come as routers, computers, or other communication devices through configurations. With firewalls, one can define the accesses which will be permitted into a particular network. User requests should be screened so as to know whether they are coming from a previously defined IP address. Telnet access into organizations should also be inhibited.

The follow are the other techniques through which you can stay secure from cyber terrorism:

1. All accounts must have passwords, and the passwords should be hard to guess.

2. The network configurations should be changed whenever the defects are known.

3. Liaise with the vendors for patches and upgrades.

4. Check logs and audit systems to detect and trace any intruders.

5. In case you receive an email message from a suspected email address, then don't open the message.

For you to stay protected against cyber-terrorism, you need to use multiple security mechanisms. Whenever you suspect that an attempt to intrude into your systems was made, then the appropriate action should be taken

Conclusion

This marks the end of this book. Each organization, local government, and state should use all the measures discussed in this book in a bid to remain protected against cyber-attacks. The protection mechanisms should be implemented on the computer hardware, software, and networks. If any of these is not well protected, then attackers can take advantage of that and gain access into the systems of the organization. The documents of an organization, both soft and hard copies, carry very sensitive information. These documents are very crucial for the operations of the organization to run smoothly. They should stay protected against attacks. Proper mechanisms should be used in a bid to ensure that these documents remain confidential, available, and unmodified by unauthorized individuals.

The computer networks should be protected against intrusion attacks. Attackers should be barred from intruding into the network systems. Data being transmitted over the network should be encrypted using the necessary techniques so that it cannot be read by unauthorized parties. If the encryption keys are to be exchanged over the network, they should be encrypted. Firewalls should be used to filter the traffic which enters or leaves an organization. This way, it will be hard for cyber-attackers to gain access into an organization via their network.

Countries should come together and partner to fight cyberwar. If not careful, cyberwar can lead to physical warfare. Cyberwar attacks can only be eliminated through a global approach.

www.ingramcontent.com/pod-product-compliance
Lightning Source LLC
Chambersburg PA
CBHW060933050326
40689CB00013B/3074